What's Your Job?

About Wise & Wide

- A systematic 6-level English reading program based on Lexile® measures
- Diverse and interesting topics chosen from the elementary curriculums of Korea and English speaking western countries
- Well-written books in various forms including fiction stories, descriptive texts, and classics retold
- The informative but original fiction stories grab your interest, leading to the easy and clear understanding of the educational content.
- Improve thinking skills with solid after-reading activities at all levels of the series.

Wise & Wide is a 6-level English reading program that consists of 60 books and each level is systematically divided by Lexile® measures. The Lexile® Framework for Reading is the most popular reading measuring system in American formal education curriculums and many English programs. Over 20 out of 50 states in the U.S. mark Lexile® measures directly on students' final report cards and over 300 well-known publishers adopt and use Lexile® measures.

Experience many kinds of readings written by professional writers from the U.S. and England. They used interesting topics that were carefully chosen after analyzing elementary curriculums from around the world including Korea, the U.S., England, and Australia among many others. Comprehensive after-reading activities including graphic organizers, speaking tasks, and After-reading Tests are ready for you.

Levels in the series and their corresponding Lexile® measures

Level	Lexile® measures	U.S. Grade
Level 1	Below 200L	Pre K - K
Level 2	190L - 400L	Lower Grade 1
Level 3	350L - 530L	Upper Grade 1
Level 4	420L - 650L	Grade 2
Level 5	520L - 940L	Grade 3 - 4
Level 6	830L - 1070L	Grade 5 - 6

* Smart Readers: Wise & Wide level 1 is applicable to the preschool level in the U.S.
* The source of the relationship between Lexile® measures and U.S. school grades: CCSS(Common Core State Standards) FOR ENGLISH LANGUAGE ARTS, APPENDIX A (2012, which is used by 45 states in the U.S.)

Topic List

	Level 1	Level 2	Level 3	Level 4	Level 5	Level 6
Book 1	Science>Biology: The hibernation of animals Story	Science>Biology: Living and nonliving things Story	Science>Biology> Animals & the Environment: Sea otters Story	Environment> Living with nature: The diver & the persimmon tree Story	Science>Biology> Animal: Amazing animals of the Amazon Story	Science>Biology: Germs, transmitted diseases Story
Book 2	Literature> World classics: Aesop's fables Story	Literature> Traditional fairy tale: Old tales about stones Story	Social Studies> Economy: To run a business to make and save money Story	Science>Biology> Plants: Photosynthesis Story	Science>Earth science: Earth's layers, earthquakes, volcanoes, and earth's atmosphere Report	Mathematics> Sequence: The golden ratio & the Fibonacci sequence Story
Book 3	Science>Physics: How shadows are formed Story	Literature> World classics: Peter Pan Story	Science>Scientific technology: Nanobots Story	Literature>Myths: World's creation stories Story	Literature> Legend: The story of King Arthur Story	Literature>Myths: Constellation myths Story
Book 4	Literature> Traditional literature: The Talmud Story	Science>Biology> Animal: Polar bears Story	Science>Biology> Animal: Mountain gorillas Story	Social Studies> Cultural anthropology: Amazing ancient cultures of the world Story	Science> Earth science: Clouds and weather Story	Literature> Human & animals: The friendship between a girl and a horse Story
Book 5	Social Studies> Ethics: Rules in daily life Story	Science>Biology: The five senses Report	Social Studies> Cultural anthropology: Astonishing festivals Report	Art>Music: Stories from two operas Story	Social Studies> World culture & history: The Renaissance Story	Sports> Board sports: Surfing & snowboarding Story
Book 6	Social Studies> World geography & travel: Tourist attractions around the world Story	Science>Biology> Animal: Dinosaurs Story	Science> Astronomy: The solar system Story	Social Studies> People: Three great people who overcame hardships Story	Science>Scientific technology: The wonderful world of robots Report	Art>Music: Composers of the Romantic Era Report
Book 7	Science> Space science: The life of astronauts Report	Social Studies> Cultural anthropology: Mythological monsters from around the world Report	Mathematics> Elementary mathematics: Numbers, measurement, shapes and data Report	Science & Social Studies> Technology & culture: Inventions from around the world Report	Art>Works of art: Famous paintings Report	Social Studies> Human & animals: Animals in action for human Report
Book 8	Social Studies> Cultural anthropology: Various living cultures of the world Story	Art>Music: Instruments in the orchestra Story	Social Studies> Life safety: Learning and using outdoor survival skills Story	Social Studies> History: The California Gold Rush Report	Social Studies & Science> Psychology: Psychology in everyday life Story	Literature> World classics: The Merchant of Venice Story
Book 9	Social Studies> Jobs: Interviews about jobs Report	Science>Scientific technology: Developments in technology in different times Story	Social Studies> Politics>Election: Running for 3rd grade class president Story	Literature> World classics: Stories of Sherlock Holmes Story	Literature> World classics: Adrift in the Pacific Story	Social Studies> History & People: Great world leaders in history Report
Book 10	Literature>Traditional fairy tale: Eastern and Western folk tales on the same theme Story	Sports>Winter sports: Various aspects of some Winter Olympic sports Report	Literature> World classics: Short stories by O. Henry Story	Sports> Ball games: Various aspects of popular ball games Report	Social Studies> History: Famous events that changed world history Report	Art & Social Studies> Art: Stories about the creation, distribution, and preservation of paintings Report

* 10 books in each level will be published.

How to Use This Book

•Before Reading

You can easily find the topic and what kind of story you are about to read.

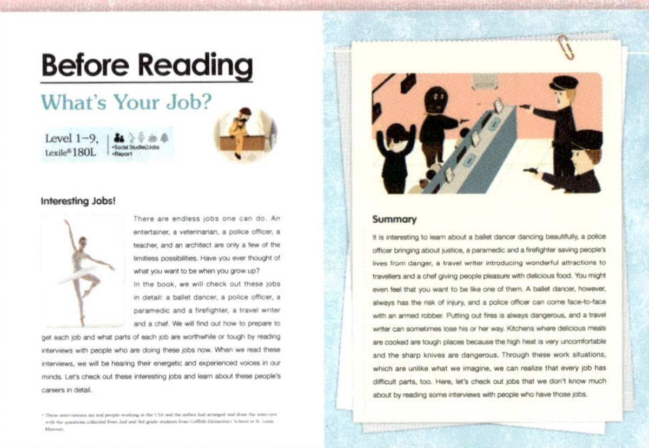

•The text

All the stories were written by professional writers from the U.S. and England, so you will read authentic and appropriate English sentences and expressions in every book in the series.

•Pop Quiz

Check out right away if you understand what you have just read by solving a pop quiz that checks your comprehension.

•Key Words

The key words and expressions on each page are listed for you to easily study them.

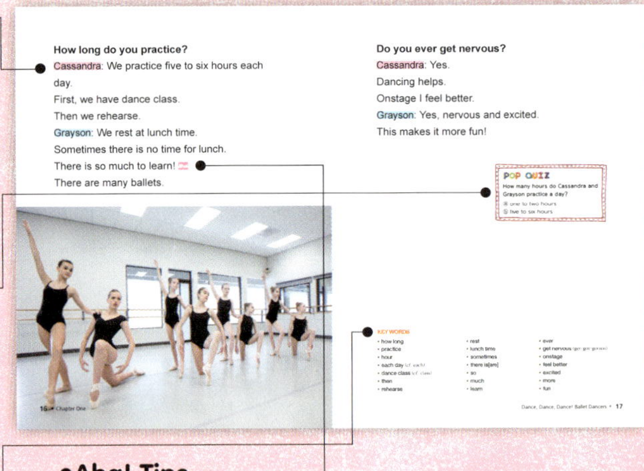

•Aha! Tips

Download free Korean explanations at *www.ihappyhouse.co.kr* for all of the sentences marked with "Aha!". These explain cultural, scientific, and economic knowledge or they deal with aspects of English such as grammatical structures or idiomatic expressions. There are lots of "Aha! Tips" to help you understand the text.

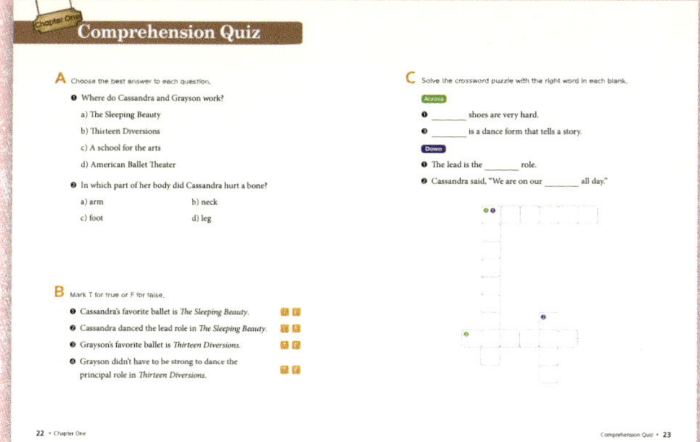

•Comprehension Quiz

After reading one chapter, solve various questions to find out if you fully understand the content.

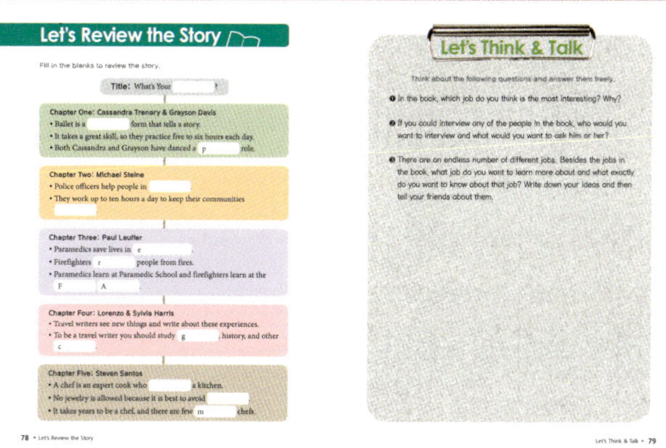

•Let's Review the Story / •Let's Think & Talk

Fill in the blanks in the organizer to summarize the whole story. Express your own thinking and feelings about the story by answering the questions. You can build up logic and reasoning skills for your essay examinations in the future.

Appendix

Audio CD

In the CD audio book form, the texts are read vividly by American professional voice actors. (MP3 files downloaded for free)

After-reading Test

Solve an additionally provided After-reading Test for each book.

The Korean translation, Answer Keys, a Word Quiz, a Word List, and Aha! Tips for each book

You can download them for free at *www.ihappyhouse.co.kr* or *www.darakwon.co.kr*

Before Reading

What's Your Job?

Level 1–9,
Lexile® 180L

• Social Studies〉Jobs
• Report

Interesting Jobs!

There are endless jobs one can do. An entertainer, a veterinarian, a police officer, a teacher, and an architect are only a few of the limitless possibilities. Have you ever thought of what you want to be when you grow up?

In the book, we will check out these jobs in detail: a ballet dancer, a police officer, a paramedic and a firefighter, a travel writer and a chef. We will find out how to prepare to get each job and what parts of each job are worthwhile or tough by reading interviews with people who are doing these jobs now. When we read these interviews, we will be hearing their energetic and experienced voices in our minds. Let's check out these interesting jobs and learn about these people's careers in detail.

* These interviewees are real people working in the USA and the author had arranged and done the interview with the questions collected from 2nd and 3rd grade students from Griffith Elementary School in St. Louis, Missouri.

Summary

It is interesting to learn about a ballet dancer dancing beautifully, a police officer bringing about justice, a paramedic and a firefighter saving people's lives from danger, a travel writer introducing wonderful attractions to travellers and a chef giving people pleasure with delicious food. You might even feel that you want to be like one of them. A ballet dancer, however, always has the risk of injury, and a police officer can come face-to-face with an armed robber. Putting out fires is always dangerous, and a travel writer can sometimes lose his or her way. Kitchens where delicious meals are cooked are tough places because the high heat is very uncomfortable and the sharp knives are dangerous. Through these work situations, which are unlike what we imagine, we can realize that every job has difficult parts, too. Here, let's check out jobs that we don't know much about by reading some interviews with people who have those jobs.

Contents

What's Your Job?

What's Your Job?

Special thanks to every interviewee and 2nd and 3rd grade students from Griffith Elementary School in St. Louis, Missouri.

Chapter One

Dance, Dance, Dance!

Ballet Dancers

Ballet is a dance form. Aha!

It takes years of training.

It takes great skill.

The dancers work in a ballet company.

They perform shows.

The dancing tells a story.

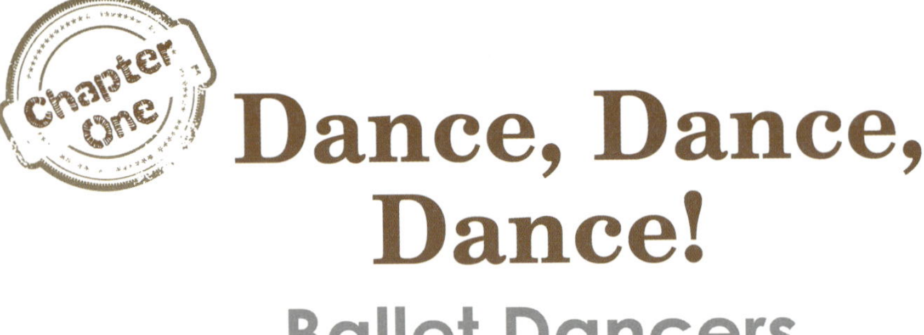

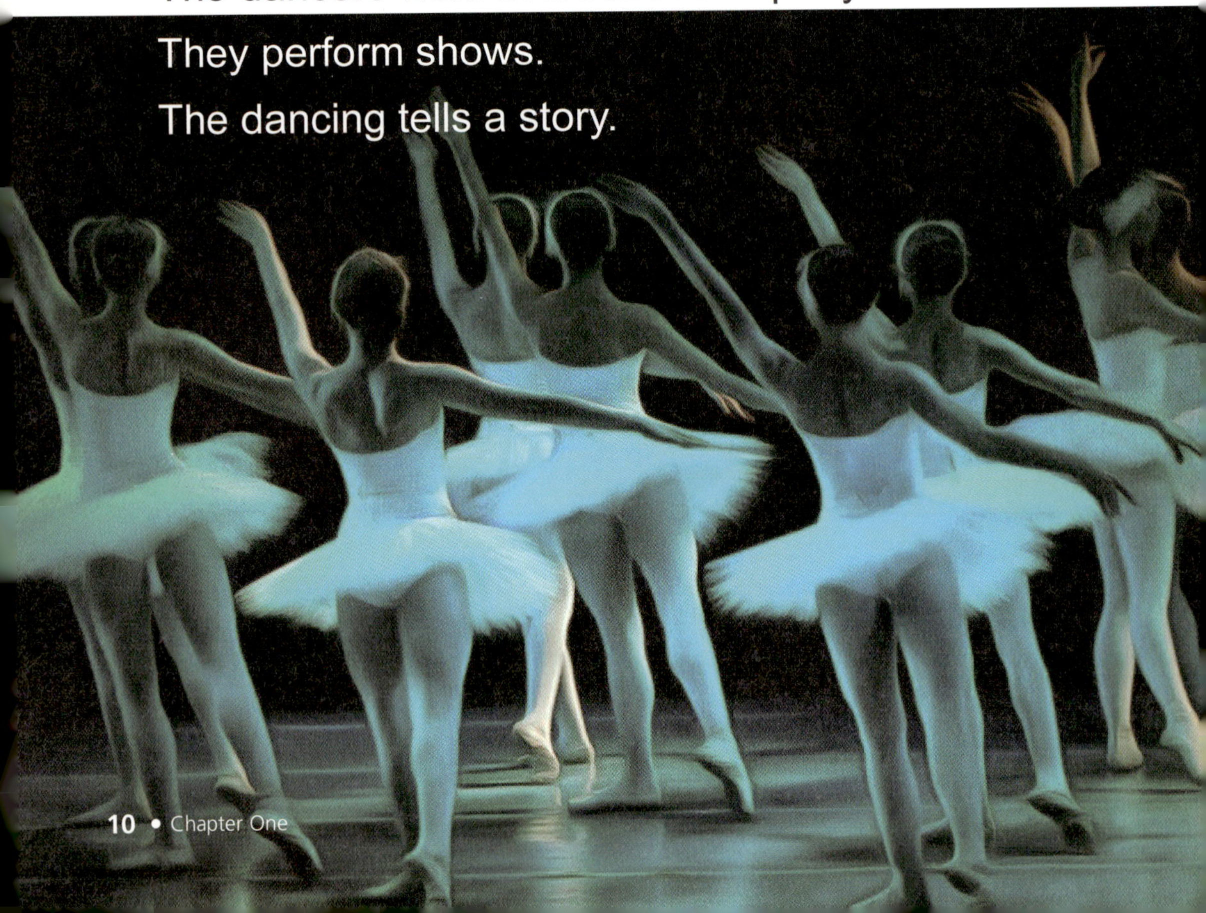

Meet Cassandra
Trenary and
Grayson Davis.
They dance with
the American
Ballet Theater.
This is in New
York City.

▲ the interviewees, Cassandra and Grayson who are
in the middle of performing (Photo by Silvia Pangaro)

What is your favorite ballet?

: The ballet is *The Sleeping Beauty*.

I danced the lead role.

The lead is the "principal role."

It is the highest rank in a company.

I loved it!

: My favorite is *Thirteen Diversions*.

It was my first principal role.

A man must be strong for this.

I felt honored to be chosen.

KEY WORDS

- favorite
- The Sleeping Beauty
- lead
- role
- principal
- highest
- rank
- love

- Thirteen Diversions (*cf.* diversion)
- first
- must + *Verb*
- strong
- feel (feel-felt-felt)
- honored (*cf.* honor)
- chosen

▲ Cassandra and Grayson who are in the middle of performing (Photos by Silvia Pangaro)

Have you been hurt dancing?

Cassandra: I am careful.

I've had many injuries.

Some in my feet.

Some in my ankles.

I hurt a bone in my foot.

I could not dance!

This made me sad.

But I had to wait.

The bone had to heal.

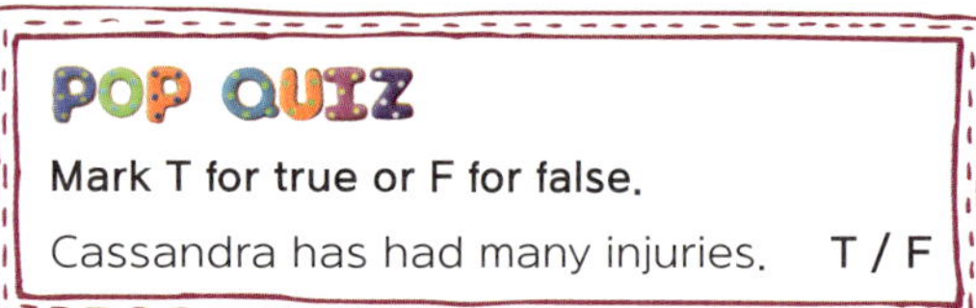

KEY WORDS

- Have you been ~?
- **hurt** (hurt-hurt-hurt)
- careful
- injury
- feet
- ankle
- bone
- could + *Verb*
- **make** (make-made-made)
- have to + *Verb*
- wait
- heal

Grayson: Yes.

I have been injured.
I once hurt my back.
It was during a show.
I kept dancing.
I was glad when the
dance ended.
I needed help!

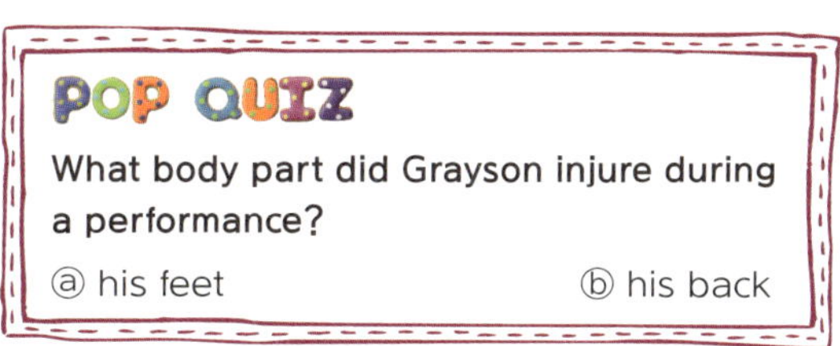

KEY WORDS

- injure
- once
- back
- during

- keep + *Verb*-ing
  (keep-kept-kept)
- glad
- when

- end
- need
- help

How long do you practice?

Cassandra: We practice five to six hours each
day.
First, we have dance class.
Then we rehearse.
Grayson: We rest at lunch time.
Sometimes there is no time for lunch.
There is so much to learn! Aha!
There are many ballets.

Do you ever get nervous?

Cassandra: Yes.

Dancing helps.

Onstage I feel better.

Grayson: Yes, nervous and excited.

This makes it more fun!

POP QUIZ

How many hours do Cassandra and Grayson practice a day?

ⓐ one to two hours
ⓑ five to six hours

KEY WORDS

- how long
- practice
- hour
- each day (*cf.* each)
- dance class (*cf.* class)
- then
- rehearse
- rest
- lunch time
- sometimes
- there is[are]
- so
- much
- learn
- ever
- get nervous (get-got-gotten)
- onstage
- feel better
- excited
- more
- fun

Does all that dancing and being on your tippy-toes make your feet hurt?

Cassandra: Sometimes.

We are on our feet all day.

Pointe shoes are very hard. Aha!

I don't notice it while dancing.

I notice it after.

That is when it hurts.

But I still love to dance!

Do you lift girls? Have you ever dropped anyone?

Grayson: The man lifts a ballerina in every ballet.
It isn't hard.
I've never dropped anyone.
I do not plan to!

◀ pointe shoes

KEY WORDS

- **tippy-toes** (*cf.* tippy)
- **on one's feet**
- **all day**
- **pointe shoe**
- **hard**
- notice
- while
- still
- lift
- drop
- anyone
- **ballerina** (*cf.* ballerino)
- never
- plan

When did you know you wanted to be a dancer?

Cassandra: I was twelve.

I took special ballet classes.

I met many great dancers.

I was asked to study ballet in New York. **Aha!**

This was amazing!

It was a great honor.

This made me believe in my dream of being a ballerina.

KEY WORDS

- **know** (know-knew-known)
- **want**
- **ask**
- **study**
- **amazing**
- **believe in**
- **dream**
- **kid**
- **make fun of**
- **because**
- **get into a fight** (*cf.* fight)
- **live**
- **town**
- **people**
- **understand**
  (understand-understood-understood)
- **art**
- **other**
- **attention**
- **no one**

Did the kids make fun of you because you did ballet?

Grayson: Yes.

Sometimes I got into fights!

I lived in a small town.

People didn't understand boys dancing.

I went to a school for the arts.

My class had no other boy dancers.

I had the attention of all the girls.

No one made fun of me then!

Comprehension Quiz

A Choose the best answer to each question.

❶ Where do Cassandra and Grayson work?

a) The Sleeping Beauty

b) Thirteen Diversions

c) A school for the arts

d) American Ballet Theater

❷ In which part of her body did Cassandra hurt a bone?

a) arm   b) neck

c) foot   d) leg

B Mark T for true or F for false.

❶ Cassandra's favorite ballet is *The Sleeping Beauty*.   T   F

❷ Cassandra danced the lead role in *The Sleeping Beauty*.   T   F

❸ Grayson's favorite ballet is *Thirteen Diversions*.   T   F

❹ Grayson didn't have to be strong to dance the
principal role in *Thirteen Diversions*.   T   F

 Solve the crossword puzzle.

Across

❶ __________ shoes are very hard.

❸ __________ is a dance form that tells a story.

Down

❶ The lead is the __________ role.

❷ Cassandra said, "We are on our __________ all day."

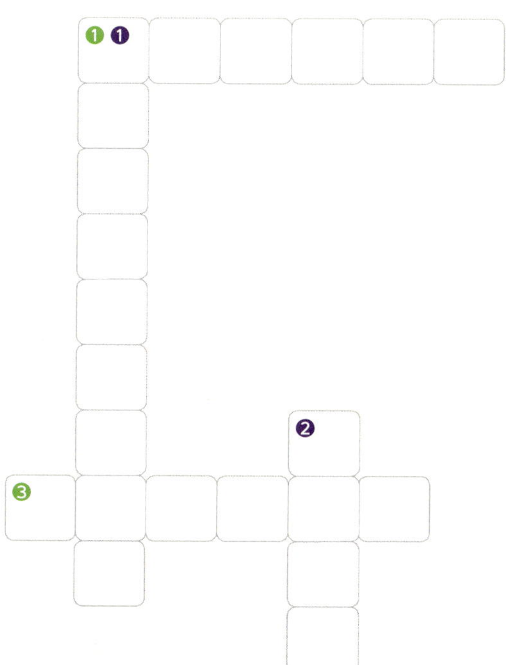

Safety First!
Police Officer

Police officers ensure people obey the laws.

They help people in need.

Police officers can be men or women.

Meet Lieutenant Michael Steine.

He is a policeman in Georgia.

This is in the United States.

Did you always want to be a policeman?

Yes!

▲ the interviewee, Michael Steine

My dad was a policeman.
I wanted to be like him.
I have been a policeman for 25 years!

KEY WORDS

- safety
- police officer
- ensure
- obey

- law
- in need
- lieutenant
- policeman

- Georgia
- the United States
- always
- for

Did you go to a special school?

Yes.

I took many tests.

Some were written.

Some were for physical fitness.

I had to pass the tests.

Then came the Police Academy.

There was much to study and learn.

I patrolled with a field training officer.

That is like an on-the-job teacher.

This all lasted many weeks.

Finally, I was a policeman!

- special school
- take a test (*cf.* test)
- written
- physical fitness
- pass
- Police Academy
- patrol

- field training officer
- like
- on-the-job
- last
- week
- finally

What do you do every day?

First, I put on my uniform.

I wear a bulletproof vest.

I carry a weapon.

I carry handcuffs and a flashlight.

I carry other things, too.

Each day is different.

▲ bulletproof vest

At work I'm told where to patrol that day.

I am told of things and people to watch out for.

I load police gear into my car.

KEY WORDS

- every day
- put on (put-put-put)
- uniform
- wear (wear-wore-worn)
- bulletproof vest
  (*cf.* bullet / bulletproof / vest)
- carry
- weapon
- handcuff
- flashlight
- thing
- too
- different
- at work
- where to + *Verb*
- watch out for (*cf.* watch)
- load
- police gear (*cf.* gear)

I load a SWAT vest.

I load a patrol rifle.

I load a gas mask.

I hope not to need
these things.
But sometimes I do.

On patrol, I respond to 911 calls.

I help people in need.

I stop speeders.

I write tickets.

I catch bad guys, like
burglars.

▲ gas mask

I work to keep my community safe.

My shift lasts ten hours each day.

There are no set breaks.

Officers eat in their cars.

We eat in a restaurant if there's time. 

POP QUIZ

Mark T for true or F for false.

Police officer stops speeders and writes tickets.   T / F

KEY WORDS

- **SWAT** (= Special Weapons and Assault Team)
- **patrol rifle**
- **gas mask**
- **respond to**
- **911**
- **call**
- **stop**
- **speeder**
- **write a ticket** (write-wrote-written)(*cf.* ticket)
- **catch** (catch-caught-caught)
- **guys**
- **burglar**
- **community**
- **safe**
- **shift**
- **set** (set-set-set)
- **break**

Are you scared of the bad guys?

No.

But some situations are scary.

We never know what is coming next. **Aha!**

That can be scary.

When you shoot someone, how do you feel?

Few officers ever have to do this.

I've only had to shoot at someone twice.

KEY WORDS

- **be scared of** (*cf.* scared)
- **situation**
- **scary**
- **shoot** (shoot-shot-shot)
- **someone**
- **few**
- **only**
- **twice**
- **bank robbery**

- **robber**
- **point at**
- **gun**
- **kill**
- **keep one's wits** (*cf.* wit)
- **follow**
- **fire**
- **hit** (hit-hit-hit)

Once was during a bank robbery.

The robber pointed his gun at me.

He said he would kill me.

I was scared.

But I kept my wits.

I followed my training.

I fired one bullet.

It hit him.

Thankfully, he did not die.

That robber caused a bad situation.

I was mad!

I didn't want to shoot him, but he would have shot me.

He might then have hurt others.

The second time was after a car chase.

My shot missed that robber.

Another officer shot him.

This robber also lived.

How do you track people down?

There are so many ways!

We use the Internet.

We track cell phones.

We track license plates.

What is the main way?

We question people who may know where the person is.

Once we tracked a person by his footprints in the snow.

We've also tracked footprints in morning dew, in the grass!

KEY WORDS

- thankfully
- die
- cause
- mad
- would have + *p.p.*
- second
- car chase (*cf.* chase)
- shot
- miss
- track + *Person/Object* + down (*cf.* track)

- way
- use
- Internet
- cell phone
- license plate
- main
- question
- footprint
- dew
- grass

Chapter Two

Comprehension Quiz

A Mark T for true or F for false.

❶ Michael didn't want to be a policeman. T F

❷ Only men can be police officers. T F

❸ Michael attended the Police Academy. T F

❹ Michael had to shoot at someone twice. T F

B Choose the best answer to each question.

❶ Who was Michael's childhood hero?

a) his mom b) his dad

c) his friend d) his brother

❷ What phone number does Michael have to answer in the patrol car?

a) 911 calls b) 411 calls

c) 888 calls d) 999 calls

C

Solve the crossword puzzle.

Across

❷ The police are trained at the Police __________ .

❸ Michael wears a bullet __________ vest.

Down

❶ I load police __________ into my car.

❹ Police officers ensure people __________ the laws.

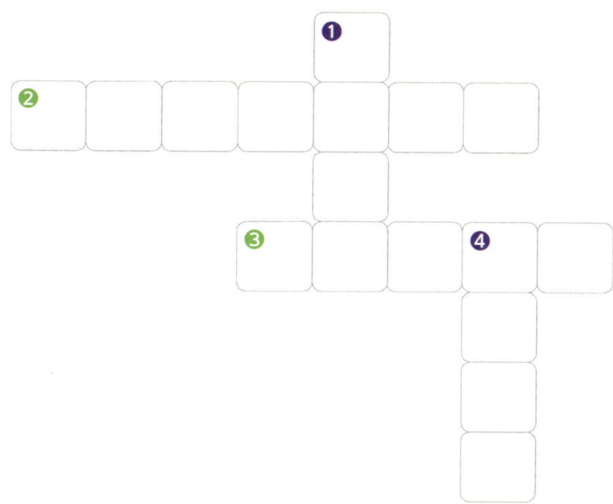

Saving Lives, Killing Fires

Paramedic / Firefighter

Paramedics are medical workers.

They save lives in emergencies.

In the U.S.A., many paramedics are firefighters.

Firefighters rescue people from fires.

They put out the fires.

Meet Paul Lauffer, a Korean American.

He is a paramedic and a firefighter in Florida.

This is in the United States.

KEY WORDS

- save
- lives
- kill the fire
- paramedic
- firefighter
- medical worker (*cf.* medical)
- emergency
- the **U.S.A.** (= the United States (of America))
- rescue
- put out
- Korean American
- Florida

Paramedic

▲ the interviewee, a paramedic and a firefighter Paul Lauffer

How do you bring people back to life?

We have learned how to help people.

We work fast.

We use medicines.

We do first aid.

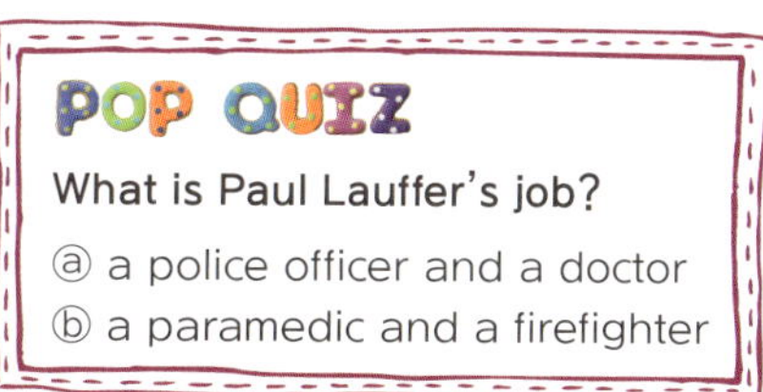

KEY WORDS

- bring ~ back to life (bring-brought-brought)
- how to + *Verb*

- medicine
- first aid

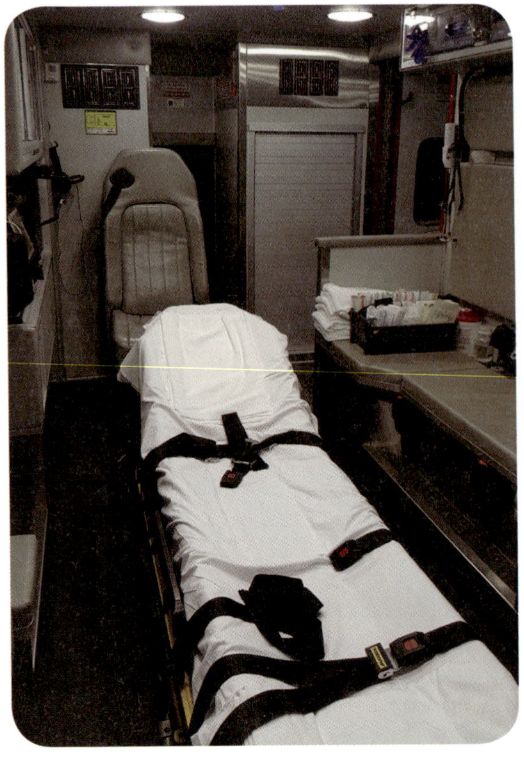

▲ inside an ambulance

We take the patient to the hospital.
We drive fast.
We drive them in an ambulance.
It is a special van.
It has medical tools.
It has sirens.
It has flashing lights.
Sirens and lights mean an emergency.
Other drivers move aside to let us go first.

- patient
- **drive** (drive-drove-driven)
- ambulance
- van
- tool
- siren
- flashing
- light
- **mean** (mean-meant-meant)
- driver
- move
- aside
- **let** (let-let-let)
- go first

How do you know what medicine to use?

We watch a patient's symptoms.

This helps us.

If their heart beats too fast?

We give medicine to slow it.

If they cannot breathe?

We give medicine to open their lungs.

- symptom
- heart
- beat (beat-beat-beaten)
- slow
- breathe
- lung

Where do you learn to be a paramedic?

Paramedics start as EMTs (Emergency Medical Technicians).

We learn basic life support.

This takes 3~4 months.

Then we go to Paramedic School.

That takes 14~16 months.

We learn advanced life support skills.

KEY WORDS

- start
- EMT
- technician
- basic life support (*cf*. basic / support)
- month

- advanced life support
- job
- agree
- see (see-saw-seen)
- make a friend

Do you like your job?

I love it!

My paramedic friends agree.

Each emergency is different.

We see new things.

People are happy that we help them.

We make new friends.

We help people feel better.

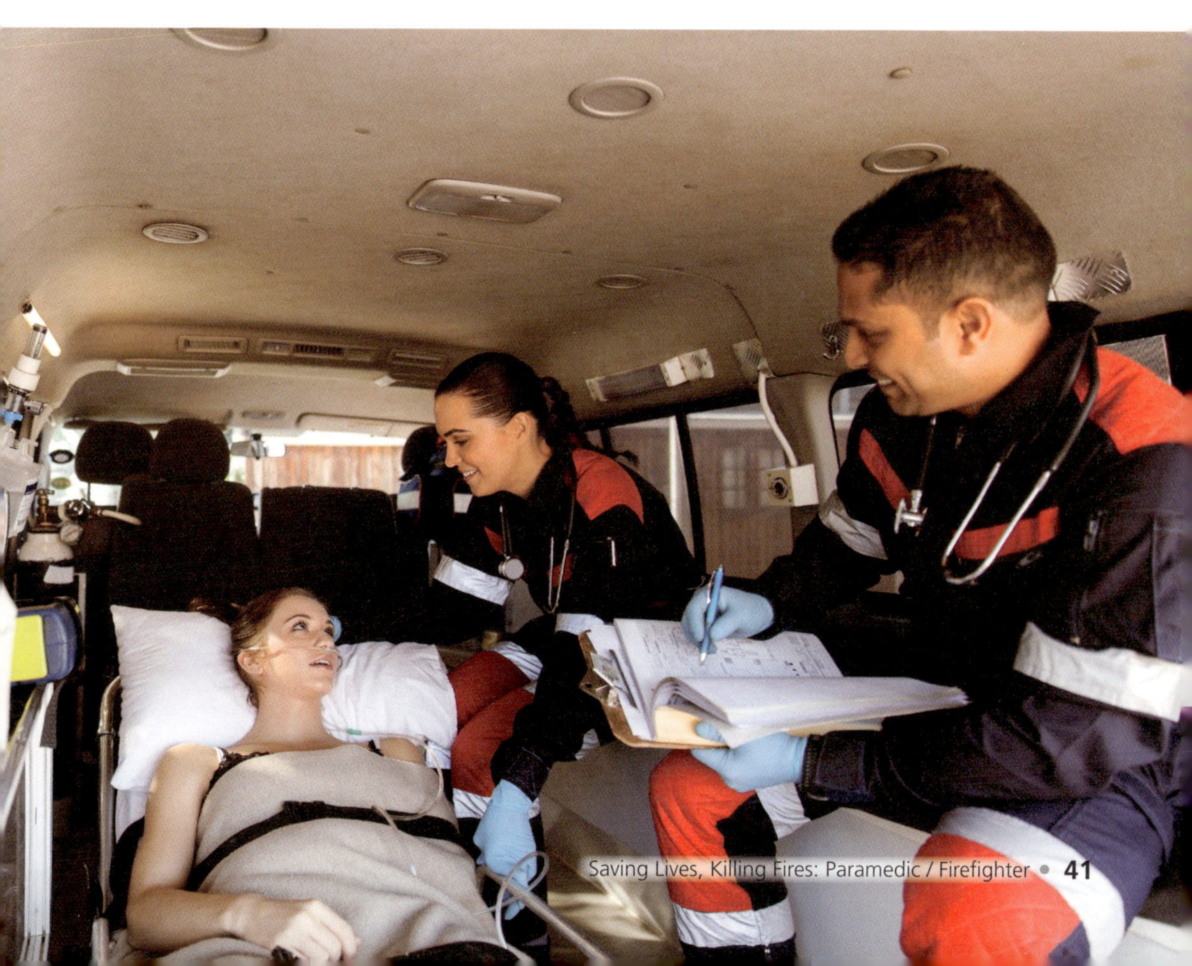

Firefighter

How do you learn firefighting?

We study at the Fire Academy.

We learn all about fires.

We learn what starts them.

We learn to put them out.

We learn safety.

We train five days a week.

We train twelve hours each day.

We do this for many weeks.

POP QUIZ

Where do people learn firefighting activities?

ⓐ the Fire Academy
ⓑ Paramedic School

- firefighting
- fire academy
- train

Is the suit hot? Is it heavy?

Yes.

It is hot.

It is heavy.

Our suit protects us.

Our gear is heavy.

So are our tools. Aha!

They can weigh 31.75 kg!

This is a lot to carry.

We must be strong.

We work hard.

We hammer.

We dig.

We crawl.

We lift heavy things.

Do you get scared?

Yes!

Fire is scary.

Backdraft is scary. 

It causes big blasts.

Flashover is scary.

This is when fire spreads fast.

Sometimes roofs fall in.

Floors fall in.

All these things are scary.

Our courage helps us.

We want to help people.

Is riding in a fire truck fun?

Yes!

It is the best feeling in the world.

Using the hose is fun too.

It is very heavy.

The water shoots out hard!

It is not like a garden hose.

Mark T for true or F for false.

Flashover is dangerous for firefighters.　　T / F

KEY WORDS

- get scared
- backdraft
- blast
- flashover
- spread
- roof
- **fall in** (fall-fell-fallen)
- floor
- courage

- **ride** (ride-rode-ridden)
- fire truck
- best
- world
- feeling
- hose
- shoot out
- garden

What if a kid makes a fake call about a fire?

Never do this!

It is very serious.

You would be in big trouble.

Firefighters must be ready to fight real fires.

Please don't waste our time this way. **Aha!**

KEY WORDS

- What if ~?
- make a call
- fake
- serious
- in trouble
- be ready to + *Verb*
- real
- waste

What if there is a real fire outside my room?

Do not open the door.

Touch the door.

Is it hot?

Then do not open it!

Is smoke coming under it?

Stuff wet clothes

under the door.

Is there a window?

Open it.

Wave.

We want to help

you.

KEY WORDS

- outside
- touch
- smoke

- under
- stuff
- wet

- clothes
- wave

Call for help.

Climb down if the drop is not too far.

Are your parents outside?

Go tell them.

Run to a neighbor.

Call 911.

KEY WORDS

- call for help
- climb down
- drop
- far
- neighbor

Are you trapped?

Crawl under your bed.

Call out!

Be loud!

Firefighters listen to hear you.

Do not be afraid.

Chapter Three

Comprehension Quiz

A Mark T for true or F for false.

❶ Paramedics do first aid.   T   F

❷ Paramedics drive slowly in an emergency.   T   F

❸ An ambulance has sirens.   T   F

❹ Paramedics start as EMTs (Emergency Medical Technicians).   T   F

B Choose the best answer to each question.

❶ What does a paramedic learn to save people's lives?

a) They learn about doctors.

b) They learn about sirens.

c) They learn about medicines.

d) They learn good driving.

❷ If there is a fire outside your room, what should you not do?

a) Open the window.   b) Open the door.

c) Hide under the bed.   d) Call for help.

  Solve the crossword puzzle.

Across

❸ Riding in the _________ is fun. (two words)

Down

❶ Firefighter's _________ protects him/her.

❷ _________ are medical workers.

❸ Never make a _________ call about a fire.

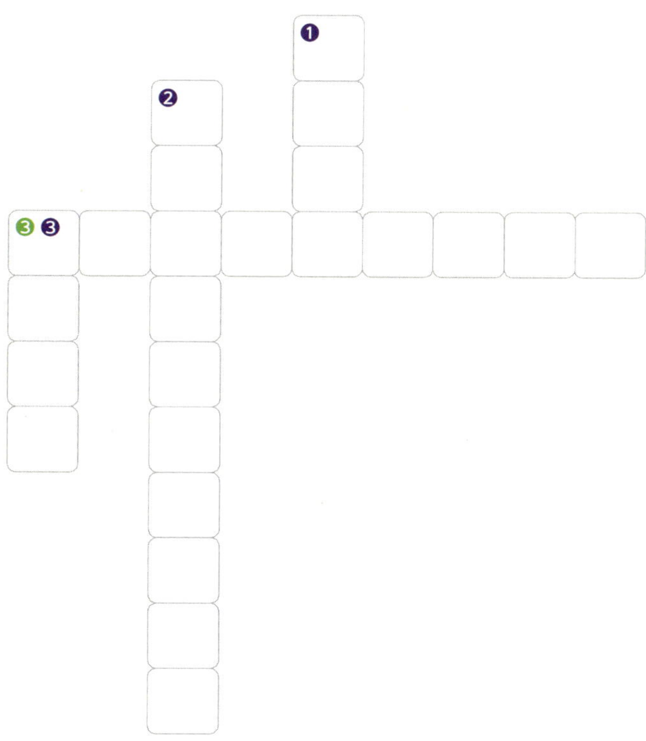

Explore the World
Travel Writers

Travel writers visit interesting places.
They meet new people.
They see new things.
They write about these experiences.
Meet Lorenzo and Sylvia Harris.

▲ the interviewees, Sylvia and Lorenzo

They are travel writers.

They have visited many places in the United States.

They wrote a book about it.

They plan to visit Europe, too!

There are different kinds of travel writers.

Some, like Lorenzo and Sylvia, visit famous landmarks.

Others travel to exotic places.

Some go on safaris.

Some explore ancient ruins.

The world is so big!

There are many places to visit.

Where would you like to go?

Where is the best place you've been?

Sylvia: The Grand Canyon.

It is in Arizona.

It is 445.78 km long.

It is 28.9 km wide.

It is over 1.6 km deep.

This trip was a dream come true!

KEY WORDS

- Grand Canyon (*cf.* canyon)
- Arizona
- one of + *Plural Noun*
- long
- wide
- over
- deep
- trip
- a dream come true

We hiked down the canyon.

This was very hard.

We grew so tired.

But we kept going!

It was so beautiful.

The colors amazed us.

We think of it often.

We have been many places.

None was greater than this.

KEY WORDS

- hike
- **grow** (grow-grew-grown)
- tired
- color

- amaze
- **think of**
  (think-thought-thought)
- often

- none
- greater
- than

How do you plan to travel?

Lorenzo: We think of many places.

We choose the most interesting one.

We read about it before going.

This way, we know what to expect.

It makes planning easier.

Planning makes the trip more fun.

Looking at maps is fun.

Learning of places to visit is fun.

We get excited about the trip.

Do you ever get lost?

Sylvia: We get lost a lot!

We don't mind.

Getting lost can be fun.

It is a good way to see unexpected things.

We use a navigation system. 

It uses the GPS
(Global Positioning
System).

It is in our car.

It directs us where
to go.

We soon find our way.

▲ navigation system

- most
- expect
- planning
- easier
- map

- get lost
- mind
- unexpected
- navigation system
- GPS

- global
- positioning
- direct
- where to go
- soon

Do you try new foods? What is the best?

Lorenzo: Yes, we are foodies.

That is someone who loves to try new foods.

It is one of our hobbies.

Our favorite is bananas foster.

This is a yummy dessert.

It is made with bananas.

It also has vanilla ice cream.

- foodie
- hobby
- banana foster

- yummy
- dessert
- be made with

- vanilla

▲ banana foster

▲ flambé

There is a special cinnamon sauce.

There is also rum.

The chef lights it on fire!

This is called flambé.

This burns away the alcohol from the rum.

It is fun to see the flambé! **Aha!**

- cinnamon
- sauce
- rum
- chef
- light (light-lit-lit)
- be called
- flambé
- burn away
- alcohol

Do you like this job? Could I do this job?

Sylvia: Yes, we love this job!

It doesn't seem like a job.

It is so much fun!

Yes, you could do this job.

Here is what you do.

Learn geography.

Learn history.

Study other cultures.

POP QUIZ

Which one did Sylvia and Lorenzo not ask
people who want to be travel writers to learn?

ⓐ geography
ⓑ driving

KEY WORDS

- seem like
- here is[are]
- geography
- history
- culture
- whenever
- foreign
- language
- writing skill
- adventure

Travel whenever you can.

Learn foreign languages.

Learn writing skills.

Write about what you see.

Write about what you do and learn.

People will read all about your adventures!

Comprehension Quiz

A Mark T for true or F for false.

❶ The Grand Canyon is in France.   T   F

❷ Sylvia and Lorenzo have not written a book.   T   F

❸ Sylvia and Lorenzo love their job.   T   F

❹ The Grand Canyon is over 1.6 km deep.   T   F

B Fill in each blank with the right word(s) below.

the United States   ruins   dream   unexpected

❶ To visit the Grand Canyon was a ______________ come true.

❷ Some travel writers explore ancient ______________.

❸ Getting lost is a good way to see ______________ things.

❹ Lorenzo and Sylvia have visited many places in ______________.

C Choose the best answer to each question.

❶ How do Sylvia and Lorenzo plan a trip?

a) They meet other travel writers.

b) They use the GPS.

c) They read about the place and look at maps.

d) They look at maps and the GPS.

❷ What is Sylvia and Lorenzo's favorite travel site?

a) Mount Rushmore

b) Yellowstone Park

c) New York

d) the Grand Canyon

❸ What is Sylvia and Lorenzo's favorite food?

a) vanilla ice cream

b) pizza

c) bananas foster

d) hamburger

What's Cooking?
Chef

A chef is an expert cook.

A man or woman may be a chef.

A chef runs a kitchen.

It takes years to be a chef.

Meet Chef Steven Santos.

He attended Le Cordon Bleu.

This is a cooking school.

▼ the interviewee, Steven Santos

Steven has been cooking for twenty years. **Aha!**

He loved to cook as a boy.

He knew he wanted to be a chef.

Steven loves being a chef!

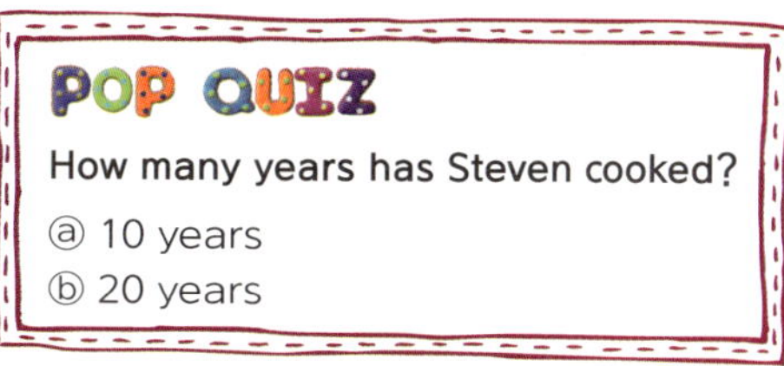

KEY WORDS

- expert
- run a kitchen (run-ran-run)
- attend
- Le Cordon Bleu
- cooking school
- cook

How can I learn to cook?

Your family can teach you.

Also there are schools.

They teach basic things.

You learn to use a knife.

You learn to cook many foods.

You learn to work with others.

You learn to run a kitchen.

You must learn on your own, too.

Practice.

Test recipes.

Make some up!

School does not make you a chef.

Training does.

Practice does.

You study with a lot of chefs.

You begin as a cook.

Later you are a sous chef.

This is a chef's helper.

After many years you may be a chef.

Six years after school I became an executive chef.

The executive chef is the kitchen boss.

- **teach** (teach-taught-taught)
- **knife**
- **on one's own**
- **recipe**
- **make up**
- **a lot of**
- **begin** (begin-began-begun)

- **later**
- **sous chef**
- **helper**
- **become** (become-became-become)
- **executive chef** (*cf.* executive)
- **boss**

To be a master chef?

You must pass tests.

These are not easy.

There are few master chefs.

It is hard to do.

You must love to cook!

KEY WORDS

- master chef (*cf.* master)
- easy
- get in the way
- be in charge
- Middle Ages
- a long time ago
- shorter
- clean
- keep A from B
- cool

Is it fun to wear the big hat? Aha!

Yes!

But it gets in the way.

The hat shows who is in charge.

It started in the Middle Ages.

That's a long time ago.

The hats were shorter then.

Hats help keep food clean.

They keep hair from food.

They look cool, too! Aha!

Do rings get in the way?

No jewelry is allowed.

Germs may grow.

Earrings may fall off.

Gems may fall off.

They might get into the food.

A diner might bite one.

Ouch!

Some restaurants allow plain wedding rings.

They honor the symbol.

Most do not allow even wedding rings.

It is best to avoid germs!

How do you chop things so fast?

I trained.

I practiced.

I chopped a lot of things.

Most chefs chop without even looking!

But chefs are careful.

To use a knife safely takes practice.

Chefs chop all the time.

Is there a food you don't like to cook?

No.

I like all foods.

I love to cook new foods.

A chef learns new things every day.

It is fun!

What happens if the power goes out?

Ice packs go on the food in coolers.

Ice helps keep food fresh.

If the power is out long?

A huge freezer truck is used.

It is like a freezer.

The food goes into the truck.

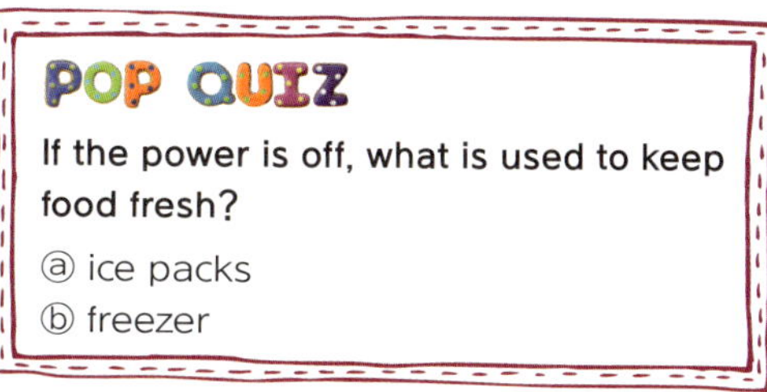

KEY WORDS

- happen
- power
- **go out** (*cf.* out)
- fresh

- ice pack
- cooler
- huge
- **freezer truck** (*cf.* freezer)

What is the hardest part of being a chef?

The easiest?

Kitchens are hot!

This is not comfortable.

Chefs work long hours.

Knives are sharp.

I have cut myself many times.

Stoves are hot.

Ovens are, too.

They might burn you.

We must be careful.

The easiest part is smiling!

When diners say, "Yummy!", this makes a chef happy.

The hard work is worth it!

KEY WORDS

- hardest
- easiest
- comfortable
- knives
- sharp
- cut (cut-cut-cut)
- many times
- stove
- oven
- burn
- smile
- be worth

Comprehension Quiz

A Mark T for true or F for false.

1. The sous chef is the kitchen boss.   T F

2. Steven loved to cook as a boy.   T F

3. Steven loves being a chef.   T F

4. The big hat shows who is in charge in the kitchen.   T F

B Fill in each blank with the right word below.

jewelry	without	Yummy	clean

1. Most chefs chop ______________ even looking.

2. Hats help keep food ____________ .

3. No ____________ is allowed in the kitchen.

4. When diners say, "____________!", this makes a chef happy.

C Solve the crossword puzzle.

Across

❸ Chefs c __________ all the time.

❹ If the power goes out, the food goes into a huge truck that is like a __________ .

Down

❶ a chef's helper (two words)

❷ A __________ is an expert cook.

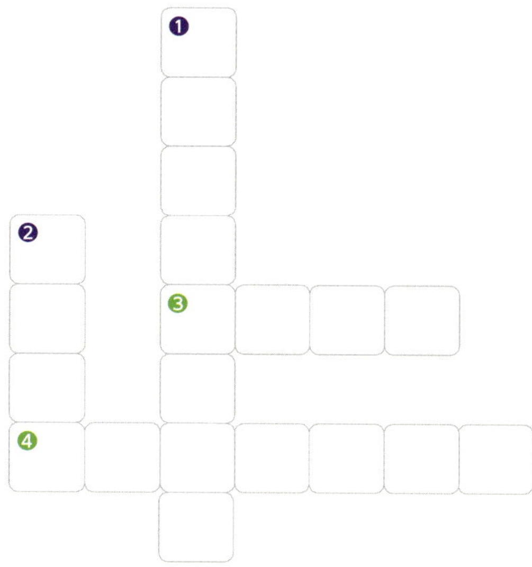

Let's Review the Story

Fill in the blanks to review the story.

Title: What's Your ____________ ?

Chapter One: Cassandra Trenary & Grayson Davis
- Ballet is a ____________ form that tells a story.
- It takes a great skill, so they practice five to six hours each day.
- Both Cassandra and Grayson have danced a p____________ role.

Chapter Two: Michael Steine
- Police officers help people in ____________.
- They work up to ten hours a day to keep their communities ____________.

Chapter Three: Paul Lauffer
- Paramedics save lives in e____________.
- Firefighters r____________ people from fires.
- Paramedics learn at Paramedic School and firefighters learn at the F____________ A____________.

Chapter Four: Lorenzo & Sylvia Harris
- Travel writers see new things and write about these experiences.
- To be a travel writer you should study g____________, history, and other c____________.

Chapter Five: Steven Santos
- A chef is an expert cook who ____________ a kitchen.
- No jewelry is allowed because it is best to avoid ____________.
- It takes years to be a chef, and there are few m____________ chefs.

Let's Think & Talk

Think about the following questions and answer them freely.

❶ In the book, which job do you think is the most interesting? Why?

❷ If you could interview any of the people in the book, who would you want to interview and what would you want to ask him or her?

❸ There are an endless number of different jobs. Besides the jobs in the book, what job do you want to learn more about and what exactly do you want to know about that job? Write down your ideas and then tell your friends about them.

Let's Review the Story

Title: What's Your **Job**?

Chapter One: Cassandra Trenary & Grayson Davis
- Ballet is a **dance** form that tells a story.
- It takes a great skill, so they practice five to six hours each day.
- Both Cassandra and Grayson have danced a **principal** role.

Chapter Two: Michael Steine
- Police officers help people in **need**.
- They work up to ten hours a day to keep their communities **safe**.

Chapter Three: Paul Lauffer
- Paramedics save lives in **emergencies**.
- Firefighters **rescue** people from fires.
- Paramedics learn at Paramedic School and firefighters learn at the **Fire Academy**.

Chapter Four: Lorenzo & Sylvia Harris
- Travel writers see new things and write about these experiences.
- To be a travel writer you should study **geography**, history, and other **cultures**.

Chapter Five: Steven Santos
- A chef is an expert cook who **runs** a kitchen.
- No jewelry is allowed because it is best to avoid **germs**.
- It takes years to be a chef, and there are few **master** chefs.

Smart Readers: **Wise** & **Wide**

After-reading Test

- What's Your Job?
- Level 1
- 18 Questions

(Vocabulary 5 / Reading Comprehension 10 /

Sentence Structure & Grammar 3)

1. Which of the following has a different meaning?

① save   ② help
③ drop   ④ rescue

2. Which of the following is similar to "hurt"?

① rehearse   ② injure
③ stuff   ④ run

3. Which of the following is NOT a pair of opposites?

① fake ↔ real
② start ↔ end
③ dangerous ↔ safe
④ believe ↔ lift

4. Which pair has the wrong past tense form of the listed verb?

① grow − grew
② teach − taught
③ run − run
④ know − knew

5. What is the right word for the blank?

> Sometimes I ___________ into fights!

① got   ② needed
③ liked   ④ made

6. What shoes made ballerina Cassandra's feet hurt?
    ① pointe shoes
    ② tap shoes
    ③ sandals
    ④ sneakers

7. Which one does police officer Michael NOT have?
    ① SWAT vest
    ② a patrol rifle
    ③ a gas mask
    ④ medicines

8. Which of the following has nothing to do with a paramedic?
    ① basic life support
    ② Paramedic School
    ③ American Ballet Theater
    ④ advanced life support skills

9. Which explanation is NOT related to the Grand Canyon which is travel writers
    Sylvia and Lorenzo's favorite attraction?
    ① It is in Georgia.
    ② Sylvia and Lorenzo think it was beautiful.
    ③ It is a dream come true for Sylvia and Lorenzo.
    ④ It is 28.9 km wide.

10. Where did chef Steven learn cooking?
    ① American Ballet Theater
    ② Fire Academy
    ③ Police Academy
    ④ Le Cordon Bleu

※ According to the story, choose the correct word(s) for the blank. (11~15)

11. Ballet dancing tells a ___________.

① joke   ② story
③ dance   ④ role

12. Police officers ensure people obey the ___________.

① boss   ② tickets
③ burglars   ④ laws

13. An EMT is an Emergency ___________ Technician.

① Skills   ② Fire
③ Medical   ④ Paramedic

14. Lorenzo and Sylvia have visited many places in ___________.

① the United States   ② Europe
③ Asia   ④ Africa

15. A chef is an expert ___________.

① dancer   ② cook
③ writer   ④ firefighter

※ **Choose the wrong part of the sentence. (16~18)**

16.

There <u>is</u> <u>so much</u> <u>learning</u>!
  ①   ②   ③   ④

17.

<u>It</u> <u>is</u> <u>fun</u> <u>seeing</u> the flambé!
① ② ③   ④

18.

<u>They</u> <u>look</u> <u>to</u> <u>cool</u>, too!
 ①   ②   ③ ④

Lisa Ricard Claro
Lisa Ricard Claro is an award-winning short story author with published articles and stories spanning multiple media, including two adult fiction novels and third scheduled for publication. She resides in Atlanta, Georgia with her husband, two dogs and two cats, and dreams of one day living at the beach. Writing is Lisa's passion, and she loves creating fiction and nonfiction stories for both adults and children.

What's Your Job?

Written by Lisa Ricard Claro
Illustrated by Sohyeon Kim

First Published in May 2017

Editorial Manager: Juyon Choi
Editors: Jiyeong Park, Kyunghee Jang
Designers: Eunhee Lee, Elim
Cover Designer: Eunhee Lee

Published and distributed by

Happy House

Darakwon Bldg., 64-1 Jandari-ro, Mapo-gu, Seoul, Korea 04031
Tel: 82-2-736-2031(ext. 250)   Fax: 82-2-732-2037
Homepage: www.ihappyhouse.co.kr
Publisher: Kyudo Chung

ISBN: 978-89-6653-525-5 18740 / 978-89-6653-156-1 18740(set)

[Components]
• 1 Audio CD (Recording Studio: Aram)
• Answer Keys & Korean Translation: Free download at www.ihappyhouse.co.kr